Financial WISDOM
COLORING BOOK
FOR
KiDS AND PARENTS

Teaching Your Children to Win
The Money Game™

Introducing... Super C.E.O. Mouse

For more information about our unique approach to teaching financial literacy to kids, teens and adults, please give us a call at 805-957-1024 or visit us on the web at www.CreativeWealthIntl.org

Created by: Elisabeth Donati & Steve Gordon

Guest Editor: Jan K. Ruskin

Illustrated by: Shayla Gordon

OUR OTHER PROGRAMS...

Camp Millionaire™ for Kids & Teens
Moving Out! for Teens
Creative Wealth Intensive
Creative Wealth for Women
Creative Cash for Kids
Creative Wealth Train-the-Trainer
Creative Wealth Licensing Program
Life's Little Wealth Principle Cards & Workbook
The Ultimate Allowance Book
The Money Game™ - *Coming Soon!*
Rocks to Riches - *Coming Soon!*

Creative Wealth™
International, LLC
Financial Paradigm Tools for the Whole Family

135 Chapala Street • Santa Barbara, CA 93101
800-928-1932 • 805-957-1024 • Fax 805-957-0125
www.CreativeWealthIntl.org • info@CreativeWealthIntl.org

Contents

"Congratulations!"

The following 26 Creative Wealth Principles evolved out of our unique and effective Camp Millionaire™ program for kids and teens.

The key to becoming financially free isn't rocket science, but it does take the knowledge and use of several very simple money management habits and wealth creation principles.

The 26 principles in this coloring book are how financially free people win The Money Game. In other words, they are the Rules to the Money Game and the earlier we learn and apply these rules, the earlier we become financially free.

You hold in your hand the first step for empowering children—yours, theirs and everyone's—with the tools they need to grow up financially free.

Our definition of financial freedom: when the passive income from your assets exceeds the expenses of your chosen lifestyle.

Our philosophy is this...

The sooner you become financially free, the sooner you have extra money to go out into the world and do more good. And isn't that what makes us all happy inside?

May you and yours enjoy coloring in this book as much as we enjoyed creating it for you.

How to Use this Coloring Book to Raise Money Savvy Adults!

Each page is designed to help you start a conversation about specific aspects of money. We've given you some ideas of what to talk about, but don't stop there. Let the child know it's okay to ask questions about money; let them learn that taking care of their money wisely is like brushing their teeth...it's just something you do to be a responsible adult.

Sit down with your child and his favorite crayons, pencils or markers and turn to any page that interests him. First, read the left hand page to yourself, and then explain it to your child as he colors the opposite page. We encourage you to color the smaller picture on the left hand side if you want (if your child will let you)! Kids love doing things with adults so just get in there and have some fun.

We know that some of the concepts will be advanced for your child ~ maybe even new to you. This book is meant to prompt the communication between you so anything goes ~ money related or not! Let the conversation lead you and, no matter what, enjoy this time together.

If your child isn't writing yet, feel free to help fill in the blanks.

We hope this ends up being one of your child's most valuable coloring books.

Enjoy!

Elisabeth, Steve, Shayla, Jan and the rest of our Creative Wealth Team worldwide.

Being financially free means you have more than enough money coming in each month from passive income than you have going out in expenses.

It means you don't have to work for the rest of your life unless you want to.

Everyone has the option of choosing to be financially free, yet many people don't choose it because no one ever tells them they have the OPTION to choose it.

Choosing to grow up financially free means you know how you want to live your life and you take a few steps toward creating that life every day.

Whose choice is it to be financially free? _____

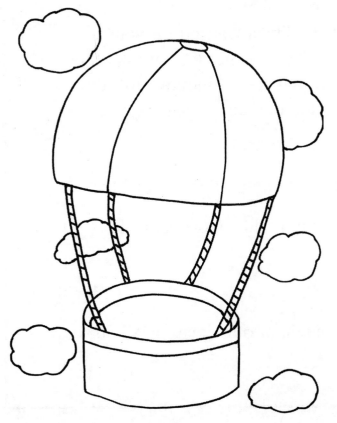

What will you do with your life when you don't have to work; in other words, when you're financially free? _____

_____

_____

_____

_____

_____

_____

Teaching Tip: ask your child how he'd like to live when he grows up.

Financial freedom is your CHOICE.

Assets are things you own that put money INTO your pocket. Assets are things like businesses, stocks, and real estate. A website that makes you money is an asset. Even books and ideas can be assets.

Assets feed us because, when we have enough of them, we are financially free to live the way we want to!

Most people buy things called **Liabilities** and liabilities take money OUT of our pockets. We like to call this stuff Piddlyjunk!

Liabilities don't feed us...they eat us. This doesn't help us become financially free.

Name three assets:

Assets: _____

Assets: _____

Assets: _____

Name three liabilities:

Liability: _____

Liability: _____

Liability: _____

Teaching Tip: Help your child come up with three assets and three liabilities. Use your own experiences and share some of the things you have spent your money on.

If you're good at something, but you're not a very nice person, what will others think about you?

Would you rather be known as a talented person who isn't very nice or a person with good character and great habits who does good things in the world?

What kinds of things are you good at?

_____

_____

What are some traits that make you the type of person others would look up to and want to be around? (Things like being honest, being on time, helping around the house without being asked, etc.)

_____

_____

_____

_____

_____

Teaching Tip: Ask your child to name qualities and character traits of people they know.

The Judge

People aren't judged by their ABILITIES but by the sum of their CHOICES.

If you live long enough and

take good care of yourself, you will eventually be an elderly man or woman. When that time comes you might not want to have to work for money anymore.

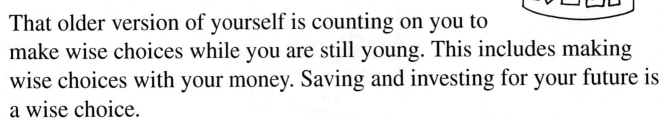

That older version of yourself is counting on you to make wise choices while you are still young. This includes making wise choices with your money. Saving and investing for your future is a wise choice.

What are some ways you can start setting money aside for YOUR older self?

_____

_____

_____

_____

_____

Teaching Tip: Ask your child what life might be like WITH plenty of money versus WITHOUT enough money.

It's not how much
money you MAKE that's
important, it's
how much you KEEP.

Did you know that if you started wisely investing $15 a week in the stock market when you're 15, this money <u>could</u> grow to over a **MILLION DOLLARS** by the time you turn 60 years old?*

What would you do with **A MILLION DOLLARS?**

_____

_____

_____

What would you do to help others with part of your million dollars? _____

_____

_____

_____

Teaching Tip: Ask your child if they know someone who does a lot of good in the world or constantly helps others. Ask him how he feels about that person. Ask him if he'd like others to feel that way about him.

---

* NOTE: The stock market is just one place to invest your money and not everyone makes money in the stock market. There are potential risks that go along with every potential reward. Education is one way of reducing or minimizing your risks when you invest.

Here's the math: $15 per week (figured as $60 per month) x 52 weeks x 50 years with a 10% return (which is possible with the right investment strategies) will give you approximately $1,193,495!

Save EARLY,
Save OFTEN,
Invest WISELY.

What would happen if you put all of your eggs in one basket and you dropped the basket?

Investing your money into one kind of asset or investment is like that basket of eggs. It's important to put your money in different investments so if one doesn't do well, you don't lose all of the money you've worked so hard to save up and invest for your future.

Putting your financial eggs in several different baskets is called

Diversification. Do you remember what an asset is?

Name a few types here:_____

_____

_____

Stocks   Real Estate   Business

Teaching Tip: Ask your child if he knows someone who owns a business, has stock in the stock market or owns real estate.

Note: Don't let the big words get in your way. When we learn a new language, it can be fun to count the letters in a word or say it in funny ways. You can also relate the concept to your life at home.

Don't put all your financial EGGS into one BASKET.

You are responsible for your thoughts. It may seem complicated, but this is how it works:

It all starts with these things called Beliefs. Your beliefs form your Thoughts. Your Thoughts lead to Feelings. Your Feelings lead to your Actions (and choices). Finally, your Actions and choices lead to your Results.

What are the results? The results are YOUR LIFE!

Your thoughts are the most powerful things you have. Watch your thoughts because whatever you think about just may happen.

When you think mostly positive thoughts, your life is mostly positive.

When you think mostly negative thoughts, your life is mostly negative.

Thoughts Become Things

What kinds of thoughts do you think most of the time? _____

_____

_____

_____

_____

Teaching Tip: Ask your child if he has friends who are mostly positive or mostly negative.

Ask him how he feels when he's around those friends. Explain positive and negative in greater detail.

Your thoughts, beliefs and attitudes determine your WEALTH potential.

Many wealthy people have been broke at some time in their lives. Wealthy people think big and aren't afraid to take actions to make their dreams come true. Rich people rarely give up.

Poor people often let a little failure stop them from reaching their goals.

Wealthy people don't let failure get in their way. To people with a wealthy state of mind, a failure is simply a learning experience and a stepping stone towards success. Each failure is simply another way something didn't work and one step closer to the way something WILL work.

What are some thoughts poor people might think?_____

_____

_____

What are some thoughts financially free people might think? _____

_____

_____

_____

_____

_____

_____

Teaching Tip: Ask your child about the last time he gave up on something. Ask him why he gave up. If he's never given up on anything, ask him what motivates him to keep going.

Being BROKE is a temporary financial condition, being POOR is a state of mind.

Money doesn't make you good or bad, it just gives you the ability to buy the things you need and want.

The more money you have, the quicker and easier you can reach your goals and dreams AND the more you can help others.

What are some of YOUR goals and dreams? Remember to dream big!

_____
_____
_____
_____

What are some ways YOU'D like to help others or the world?

_____
_____
_____

Teaching Tip: Share some of your own goals and dreams with your child. Sometimes children only see us working and don't know what we're working towards.

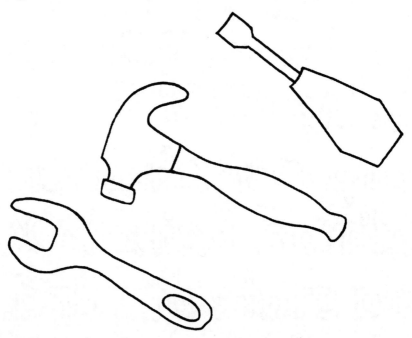

Money is a TOOL to reach your DREAMS.

Wealthy people invest in assets

which increase in value over time and/or pay them passive income so they can eventually work because they WANT to and not because they have to. Some assets don't create passive income but do still grow in value over time.

When YOU start investing your money in assets, it will be working for you, too.

How can YOUR money work for you?

_____

_____

_____

Teaching Tip: Talk to your children about people they know who are retired and living off of the passive income from their assets (this MAY be you). Ask them if they would like doing the same thing when they are older.

Note: This may be a good opportunity to ask your child to identify some of his gifts, skills and things he likes to do. You can lay the foundation for creating work or jobs that will be fulfilling and satisfying later on.

To create FINANCIAL FREEDOM, invest the ENERGY of money wisely.

In order to make money grow, you have to put it to work for you instead of wasting it. You put it to work for you by investing it and you waste it by spending it on Piddlyjunk.

Money is like energy. Maybe that's why we call it currency!

You can USE the energy in your money or you can waste it. It's totally up to you.

What are some ways to invest the energy of YOUR money? _____
_____
_____
_____

Teaching Tip: Help your child name things that go UP in value and things that go DOWN in value.

GO UP   GO DOWN

Make money GROW by putting it to WORK for you.

Where do YOU want to go in life?

You can take your life anywhere you want. But it can only take you there if you KNOW where you want to go.

Imagine going on a vacation. Unless you know where you're going, you don't know what to pack, how much money to take, whether you need a passport or which direction to drive or fly.

Where do YOU want to go?

_____

_____

_____

_____

Teaching Tip: As a family, sit down with a world map and talk about all of the places you'd like to go. Then talk about what you'd need to take with you to the different places. Look at how the list of things you'd need to take might change depending on where you choose to go.

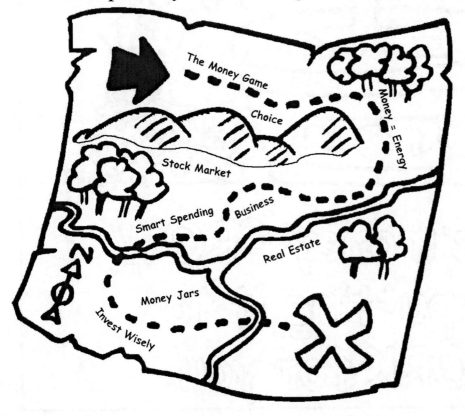

If you don't know where you're GOING, any road will TAKE you there.

Most people who have succeeded

originally set out with a plan. They knew where they were going, figured out how to get there and then took action steps to reach their goals.

Most people who do NOT succeed don't take the time to figure out what they want or to write out a plan.

What is one of your goals? _____

How do you plan on reaching this goal?_____

_____

_____

_____

Teaching Tip: Share one of your personal goals with your child, the plans you made and the steps it took to reach that goal.

Now help your child decide on a short-term goal, create a plan and write out the steps he needs to take to reach that goal.

When your child talks about wanting to do something in the future, remind him about creating a plan first.

Most people don't plan to FAIL; they fail to PLAN.

Words for Puzzle 1

ACROSS

3 Financial _ _ _ _ _ _ _ _ is your choice. You reach financial _ _ _ _ _ _ _ _ when your passive income is greater than your living expenses.

4 It's not how much _ _ _ _ _ you make that's important, it's how much you keep.

5 Most people don't _ _ _ _ to fail; they fail to plan.

9 If you don't _ _ _ _ where you're going, any road will take you there.

12 _ _ _ _ _ _ _ _ _ _ _ take money out of your pockets.

13 Money is a _ _ _ _ to reach your dreams.

DOWN

1 _ _ _ _ early, _ _ _ _ often.

2 People aren't judged by their abilities but by the _ _ _ of their choices.

3 Don't put all your _ _ _ _ _ _ _ _ eggs in one basket.

6 When you own these, they put money in your pocket. _ _ _ _ _ _ _ feed you.

7 To create financial freedom, _ _ _ _ _ _ the energy of money wisely.

8 Your thoughts, beliefs and attitudes determine your _ _ _ _ _ _ _ potential.

10 Being broke is a tempory financial condition. Being poor is a _ _ _ _ _ of mind.

11 Make money _ _ _ _ by putting it to work for you.

> Complete the sentences on this page and then put the words on the next page.

Financial Wisdom Puzzle 1

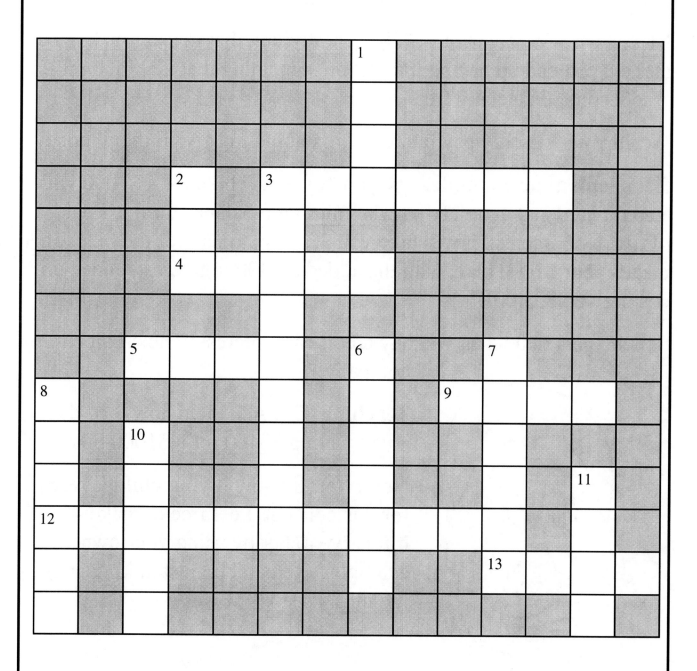

Answers on Page 76

When you put your money in a bank,

you're giving them permission to loan it out to other people to buy things like houses, cars and businesses. Those people pay the bank INTEREST on the loans and the bank pays YOU interest for letting them use your money. This is how banks make money.

BUT, if you borrow money to buy Piddlyjunk that doesn't make you money, you end up paying interest on something that isn't helping you become financially free.

Wealthy people only pay interest if it's going to MAKE them money.

Let's look at an example: Say you buy a new bike for a $1000 with a credit card and you only pay the minimum balance until it's paid off. At 18% interest, it will take you 22 years to pay for the bike. That means your $1000 bike, with the added $2,400 in interest, ended up costing you $3,400!!!

So who gets rich when you pay credit card interest? The credit card company!

Teaching Tip: Ask them how they'd feel about paying $3400 for a $1000 bike.

Note: You'll know if your child is ready for this concept. Feel free to make it relative to her by using your own examples. Remember, just talking about it plants a seed.

Interest is only INTERESTING when you're RECEIVING it.

When you borrow money, ask yourself if you are borrowing the money to make more money or borrowing the money to buy yourself more stuff?

If you're borrowing it to make more money...GREAT JOB!

If you're borrowing it to buy more stuff, chances are you will never be financially free.

If you could borrow money, what would you use it for?

What are some good reasons to borrow money?

_____

_____

_____

Teaching Tip: Talk to you child about loans you have had in the past and loans you currently have. Tell them why you borrowed the money and whether or not you would do it again. Talk about the emotions involved with borrowing money.

Note: You can always use the lemonade stand as an example. "If you borrowed money to set up a lemonade stand…"

Only BORROW money
when it's going to
MAKE you money.

Most wealthy people

pay themselves first, before paying anyone or anything else. This means that every time they get paid they put money into their own financial freedom account before they pay bills or spend money on other things.

When you have enough money saved up you can invest it (put it to work for you) so that it grows and can pay you later.

If you don't ever do this, you can never stop working because you won't have any investments that produce passive income for you to live on.

Financially free people work because they WANT to, not because they HAVE to.

If you start Paying Yourself First every time YOU get money, and learn to invest it wisely, chances are YOU can become financially free sooner than most people.

Could you start saving some money now?_____

I always pay myself first!

Teaching Tip: Talk to your child about whether or not you pay yourself first.

Tell him whether you started doing this early or later in life.

Explain how much money you'd have now if you had started earlier.

Pay YOURSELF first.

Having lots of stuff doesn't usually make people happy for very long.

True happiness comes from having people in your life who love you, plenty of friends, and joyful experiences.

Did you know people with a lot of money can be unhappy and people with very little money can be very happy?

What kind of stuff did you think would make you happy before you bought it but after awhile really wasn't that big of a deal after all?

_____

_____

_____

What are some things or experiences that might bring you happiness?

_____

_____

_____

Teaching Tip: Ask your child about the 'stuff' in his life. Talk about how long it took for the newness to wear off.

Also, talk about the fact that we usually buy things because of how we think those things are going to make us feel. Ask him how he felt the last time he bought something or you bought something for him.

Money buys you STUFF, not HAPPINESS.

Who is the C.E.O.? The Boss!

C.E.O. is short for Chief Executive Officer.

Did you realize that you are the C.E.O. of your own life? Yup. You are the boss. The way your life turns out is up to you.

Life is a do-it-yourself project. Of course there are people who influence your life but it's you who will ultimately succeed based on your own efforts.

When would you like to start working on YOUR life? After all, if you don't do it, who will?

Are you ready to put on YOUR C.E.O. hat? _____

What are some ways that you are already responsible for your life?

_____

_____

Where have you not been responsible for your own life?

_____

_____

_____

_____

_____

_____

Teaching Tip: Talk about how it feels to be in charge of your life versus letting someone else be in charge. Ask your child which one they'd prefer and why.

42 - Adult's Side

You are the C.E.O. of your own life; financial freedom is YOUR responsibility.

If you can't pay for the things you want in cash, you shouldn't buy them yet!

Instant gratification means buying something RIGHT NOW instead of saving up for it.

A lot of people get into financial trouble by buying things they want with credit cards. If they don't have the money to pay the credit card bill, they end up paying interest to the credit card company. This interest can add up to a lot of money over time.

The only exception to this rule is if you borrow money to buy an asset that is going to make you money. (See Page 37)

What kinds of things could you save up your money to buy?

_____

_____

_____

Teaching Tip: Talk to your child about how long it takes to pay off credit card debt and how much more you have to pay because of it.

Go to the web and search for "interest calculators." Explore how much you end up paying if you make minimum payments on a credit card that charges 18% interest.

If you can't afford it
in CASH, you can't
afford it at all.

If you don't keep track of your stuff it tends to get lost. Toys are like that. Money is like that.

Pay attention to your pennies because 100 pennies add up to a dollar. Know where your money is going. Only then, can you turn it into more, for now and for later.

Do you know where YOUR money goes? _____

How can you keep track of all the money you receive and all the money you spend? _____

Financially free people always know where their money is and where it's going.

If it works for them, it will probably work for you, too!

Teaching Tip: Ask your child if he has heard the word BUDGET. Then explain to him that a budget is a way to keep track of his money.

For a great budgeting and tracking website to visit with your kids, go to www.mint.com.

There is risk in just about everything. You can't avoid risk but you can educate yourself in order to manage it.

When you learn to manage risk, you'll do things like look both ways before you cross the street, put your seat belt on and eat your veggies.

The same thing goes for saving and investing money. You need to learn where the risks are and to ask successful people for advice.

What are some things you do now that might be risky? _____

_____

How do you manage those risks? _____

_____

_____

How do people learn to manage the financial risks?

(Hint: you're learning how now!)

Teaching Tip: Share with your child a time in your own financial experiences where you lost money because you didn't understand the risks involved or didn't get enough advice.

Ask your child how learning the language of money might help him understand financial risks later in life.

Financial success comes from MANAGING risk, not AVOIDING it.

Life should be fun and full of happiness.

Many people live the way they think they SHOULD instead of the way they really WANT.

Life is YOUR adventure and only you can decide how you want to live it.

Because everyone is unique and different, no two lives are the same.

How are you unique and what do you love to do? _____
_____
_____
_____

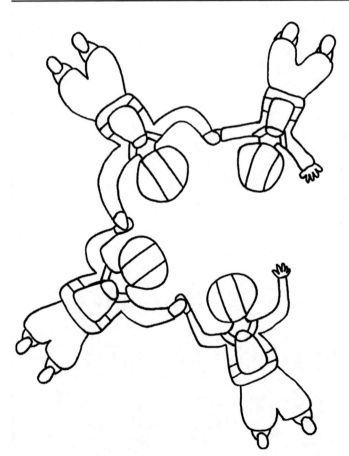

What if you could take one thing you love to do and earn money by doing it?_____
_____
_____
_____

Teaching Tip: Ask your child about the things he loves to do.

Brainstorm ways to turn that passion into a business.

Life is an ADVENTURE; let PASSION be your guide.

Everything created by humans was

someone's idea first.

Once you know what you want, follow these three simple steps to begin to create it:

1) See it in your mind.

2) Say it out loud.

3) Write it down or draw a picture of it, and put it on your wall.

Write down something you want for yourself: _____

Imagine that you already have it. Describe what you see: _____
_____
_____

Now SAY what you want as if it's already true. This is called an affirmation! Examples: "I always clean my room." "I invest my money wisely." "I appreciate my parents."

Write your affirmation here: _____

Next, create a picture of what you want.

Teaching Tip: Get a piece of poster board, some magazines, glue, scissors and a bucket of imagination and help your child create his first Dream Board.

Hey, why don't you create a Dream Board of your own right along with your child?

SEE it, SAY it,
WRITE it Down.

Stock, savings account, checking account

, assets, interest, growth fund, mutual fund, liabilities, deductions, taxes, C.E.O., cash flow, expenses, earned income, passive income, good debt, bad debt, IRA, 401K, diversification, risk and a whole lot more.

Going into the world of money is like going to a different country where you can't speak the language. It's always easier to get around if you know the language.

How will you learn the language of money?_____

_____

Teaching Tip: Go to the back of this coloring book with your child and start introducing him to the language of money.

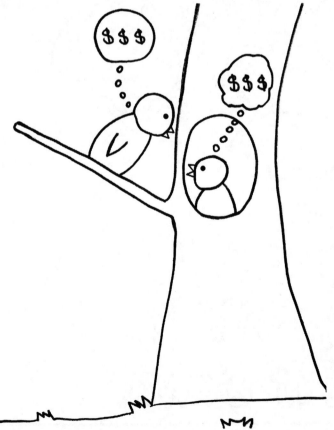

Some of the terms may seem complicated at first but, before you know it, she'll be speaking 'money' like a pro.

Then start using these financial terms in your day to day conversations with your child.

We also suggest that you point out these terms in newspaper and magazine articles.

Have fun with it!

To be financially successful learn the LANGUAGE of money.

In order to invest wisely, you need to do your research, look at what's happening in the world, pay attention to the news and learn all about the assets you're investing in.

Many people make financial decisions because they think something 'feels' like the right thing to do or they get a 'hot tip' from someone. This is NOT the way to make wise financial decisions.

What might happen if you made a financial decision based on a hot tip or a feeling not based on solid facts?

_____

_____

How can you keep from making financial decisions that cause you to lose money instead of make money?_____

_____

Teaching Tip: Share a great financial decision and a poor financial decision you made with your own money.

Ask your child if he knows of anyone or has read about people who have made poor decisions and wise decisions.

Invest with your HEAD, not with your HEART.

We all have habits that we do and habits that we don't do.

Financially free people have money habits that they developed when they were young, that helped them become financially free.

Two money habits YOU can do: always have a budget and develop a SYSTEM for managing your money.

The Money Jars are a great money habit.*

List some habits you already do with your money: _____
_____
_____

List some habits you'd like to do:_____
_____

Teaching Tip: Talk to your child about your own financial habits or those you'd like to start.

* For more info, visit: www.creativewealthintl.org/moneyjars.php

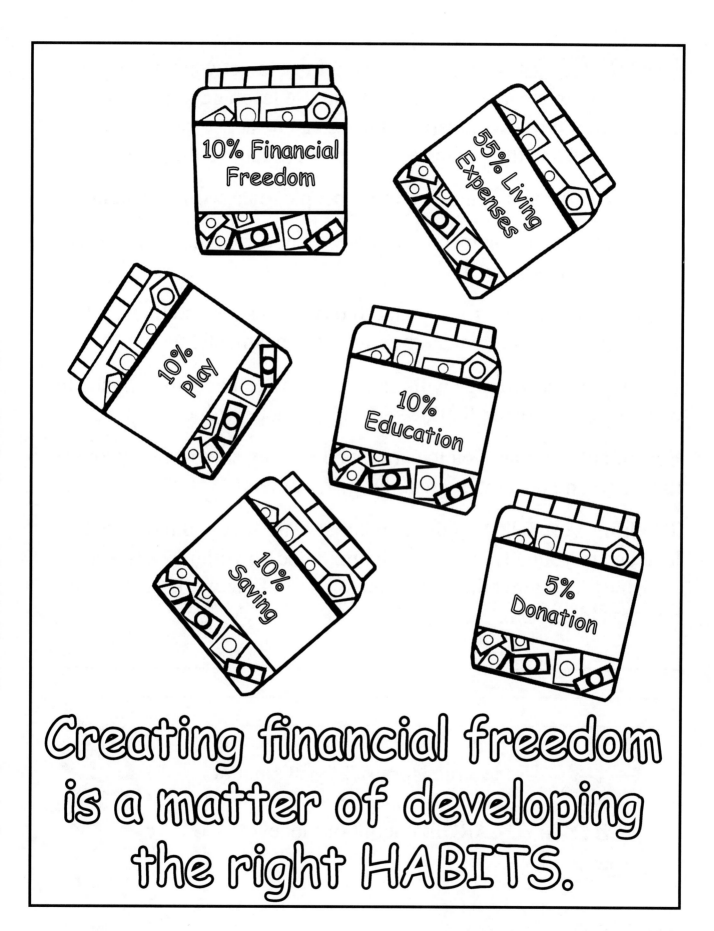

Creating financial freedom is a matter of developing the right HABITS.

Leverage is something that helps you get what you want. Financially free people understand and use leverage to their advantage. They also understand there can be added risks when you use leverage and they educate themselves to reduce these risks.

They start businesses and hire other people to do work for them.

They buy stock in companies that pay them dividends so they earn money while they sleep.

They borrow money from a bank to buy real estate and then rent it out to tenants for more than their monthly payments.

Learning to use leverage will make it so you can become financially free sooner than later. It allows you to do more with less.

Best of all? It allows you to earn lots of money so you can go out into the world and do a lot of great things for others!

Teaching Tip: Talk to your child about ways that you have used leverage to your advantage. Help him come up with ideas to start a business and hire others to do most or all of the work. List those business ideas here:

_____

_____

_____

Use leverage to turn a small amount
of money into a
LARGE amount of money!

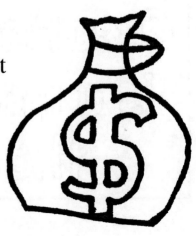

Bonus Principle!

Leverage is UTILIZING other people's time, energy and money to make YOU money.

Words for Puzzle 2

ACROSS

1   Financial success comes from managing _ _ _ _, not avoiding it.

4   To be financially _ _ _ _ _ _ _ _ _ _ _ learn the language of money.

8   Invest with your _ _ _ _, not your heart.

9   Only _ _ _ _ _ _ money when it's going to make you money.

11   _ _ _ _ _ _ _ _ is only interesting when you are receiving it.

Complete the sentences on this page and then put the words on the next page.

DOWN

1   You are the C.E.O. of your own life; financial freedom is your _ _ _ _ _ _ _ _ _ _ _ _ _ _ _ _.

2   Life's an adventure; let _ _ _ _ _ _ _ _ be your guide.

3   Money buys you _ _ _ _ _ _ , not happiness.

5   If you can't afford it in _ _ _ _, you can't afford it at all.

6   _ _ _ yourself first.

7   See it, say it, _ _ _ _ _ it down.

8   Creating financial freedom is a matter of developing the right _ _ _ _ _ _.

10   It's better to tell your money where to go than to ask where it _ _ _ _.

Financial Wisdom
Puzzle 2

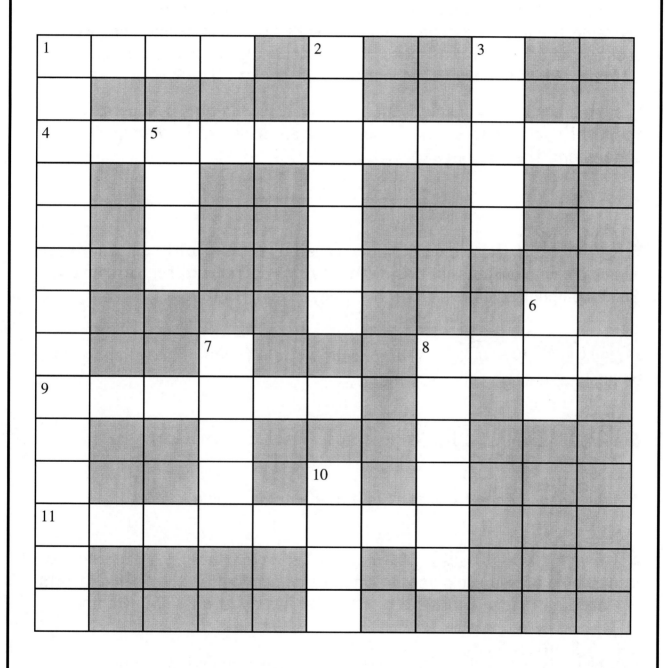

Answers on Page 77

Language of Money

If you travel to a country and don't speak the native language, it's hard to find what you need and create the experience you want to have. Learning the language of money early makes it so your child can get around the adult world of money at an earlier age and helps ensure that he knows what to do with his money when he gets it.

Yes, these may seem like advanced financial words but, if you start using them with your child, both of you will be surprised at how easy it is to understand the Language of Money.

. . . .

401 (K) - Retirement plan offered by a for-profit company that allows its employees to set aside money, tax-deferred, for retirement. Some companies will even match employee contributions.

Abundance - The concept or belief that there is enough to go around; enough for everyone.

Appreciation - Increase in value of an asset.

Asset - Something that is owned and has value.

ATM Cards (Automated Teller Machine) - A plastic card issued by a bank or to a person who has an account at that bank. It lets the account holder deposit and withdraw money at an ATM machine.

Bad Debt - When you borrow money in order to buy Piddlyjunk, in other words, stuff that doesn't make you money.

Balance - The amount of money you have in a bank account at any given time.

Bank Statement - A form you get from the bank each month that shows you how much money you have in your account as of the date on the statement, how much you put into your account that month, how much you took out of your account that month (withdrawals, checks, ATM, debit card purchases) and any fees you paid.

Bear Market - A long period of time in which stock prices fall, or remains flat, usually accompanied by widespread feelings of pessimism among investors.

Board of Directors - Individuals elected by a corporation's shareholders to oversee the management of the corporation.

Borrowing - When someone gives you something to use that you must give back.

Broke - A temporary financial condition people find themselves in when they don't have access to money.

Budget - A forecast of your income and expenses expected for some time in the future. This is also known as your SSP or Savings and Spending Plan.

Capital - Wealth in the form of cash or goods used to generate income. Also referred to a principal.

Cash - Paper money or coins that one uses to pay for things.

Cash Flow - A measure of a company's or person's financial health. Positive cash flow is when you have more money coming into your company or life than you have going out. Positive cash flow is necessary to be financially free.

C.E.O. - Stands for Chief Executive Officer; usually the president of a company, the one in charge.

Certificate of Deposit (CD) - A low risk, low return investment offered by banks and credit unions. It is also called a "time deposit" because the investor has agreed to keep the money in the account for a specified period of time. There is a monetary penalty for taking the money out before its maturity date.

Check - A form of payment for a purchase that 'tells' the person or business you wrote the check to that you have the money in your checking account. When the person or business deposits your check into their own bank account, your bank will transfer the amount of the check into their account to complete the purchase.

Collateral - Property (land, house, stocks and bonds, car, jewelry, art, etc.) used to secure or guarantee a loan. If the loan is not paid, the lender can take the property (collateral) as payment instead.

Collectibles - Items such as baseball cards, antiques, or coins that have value due to their rarity or desirability.

Compound Interest - Interest paid on the original deposit plus accumulated interest of prior periods; when your interest earns interest.

Corporation/Company - Different types of business organizations that are granted permission by a state giving it legal rights as an entity separate from its owners. It is characterized by the limited liability of its owners and the issuance of shares of stock.

Credit - Refers to the state of using other people's money.

Credit Cards - Cards used to borrow money or buy goods and services, with the promise of paying later. Credit card purchases include interest if not paid off in full by the due date each month.

Debit Cards - Similar to a check, a debit card is a promise that the recipient will be paid out of your bank account immediately and electronically. Because it is taken directly from funds in your bank account, no debt is incurred.

Debt - An IOU or an obligation to pay. Bonds are debt instruments.

Depreciation - Decrease in value of an asset.

Dividend - A portion of the profits that some companies decide to pass on to their stockholders.

Diversification - Investing in a wide variety of assets; reduces your overall risk since some investments may perform better than others at any given time.

Donation - Giving a percentage of one's income to a worthy cause, such as a church, a mission, or Green Peace. Also known as tithing, giving or philanthropy.

Down Payment - The part of the purchase price for a house/car or other large purchase that the buyer pays in cash, up front, before he obtains a mortgage or loan for the remaining balance.

Earned Income - Income from a job as an employee, also known as wages, salaries, tips, commissions, and bonuses as opposed to income from an investment. This is money you trade your time and energy for.

Expenses - Things that cost you money, i.e., in a business, expenses would include office rent, paper supplies, advertising, etc. At home, expenses would include rent or your house payment, food, insurance, gas, etc. Business expenses are often tax deductible.

Financial Freedom - When your passive income exceeds the expenses of your chosen lifestyle; not being dependent on anyone else for your financial expenses.

Financial Planner - A professional trained to help you plan and reach your long-term financial goals through investments, tax planning, asset allocation, retirement planning, and estate planning. A good financial planner should help you with Cash Flow management as well as insurance planning (to protect the downside) advice. These are just as important if not more so than investment management.

Financial Wisdom - The ability to know how to make, manage, multiply and donate your money wisely.

Good Debt - When you borrow money in order to make you money. Good debt is usually paid by someone else, e.g., the renter pays rent to live in your rental house and you in turn use that money to make the payments on your home loan.

Gross Pay - The total amount of your paycheck before taxes and other deductions are taken out.

Inflation - The term used for a rise in prices which occurs when a government puts too much money into circulation.

Insurance - A promise of compensation for specific potential future unexpected loss or injury in exchange for a periodic payment (e.g., health insurance, car insurance, home owner insurance, life insurance).

Interest - 1) A fee charged by a lender for the use of borrowed money, or 2) The return on an investment.

Investing - When you put your money to work for you (see investment).

Investment - The outlay of money to purchase assets such as stocks, bonds, real estate or a business with the objective of making a profit when sold or receiving an income from dividends, interest, or rent while it is owned.

Investor - One who makes a business of investing in stocks, real estate, business, etc.

IRA - (Individual Retirement Account) A retirement account that allows you to invest a set amount of money each year where it will earn interest and/or dividends on a tax-deferred basis.

Leverage - Utilizing other people's time, energy and money to make you money.

Liability - What you owe; a financial obligation or debt.

Loan - Money or property given to a borrower with the agreement that the borrower will return the property or repay the money, usually with interest, at a specified time.

Millionaire - A person whose net worth (their assets minus their liabilities or what they own minus what they owe) is at least one million dollars.

Money Jars - A money management system that involves dividing your money into six or more accounts: living, freedom, savings, education, play and donation. This way there is always plenty of money for everything you need and everything you want.

Needs - Things that are essential or necessary to live.

Net Pay - The amount of your paycheck after taxes and other deductions have been taken out.

Net Worth - Your total assets minus your total liabilities.

NSF - Stands for Non-Sufficient Funds. If you write a check and don't have enough money in your account to cover it, you will get an NSF notice from your bank and be charged NSF fees.

Passive Income - Income received from assets (business, stocks or real estate investments) that you don't trade your time and energy for each day. Usually requires some work but you're not 'going to work' in order to get paid.

Pension - A benefit (money or other compensation) offered by some employers and received after a person retires. These plans generally pay you a monthly income based upon your years of service with the employer.

Piddlyjunk - The stuff you buy that either goes down in value after you buy it or has no value after you buy it. It's how most people waste their money on a regular basis.

Poor - A state of mind that involves thinking one will never have enough money or be able to afford the things one wants in life.

Portfolio - A collection of all of your investments (stocks, bonds, mutual funds, real estate).

Principal - The amount of money borrowed or the part of the amount borrowed that is still owed. In investing, the principal is the amount of the original investment.

Profit - The money a business makes after it pays all its expenses. Total revenue minus all expenses equals profit.

Real Estate - Investments of land, building, houses, condos, shopping center, etc., that people invest in to create streams of passive income.

Reconcile - (same as balance) – To make sure your banking records (normally for a checking account) match your monthly bank statement.

Register - What you use to keep track of your money, e.g., checks you write, debit card purchases, deposits, withdrawals, etc. It's important to keep track of what you do with your money. If you don't, you can 'bounce' checks, forget to pay bills, etc.

Retirement - The point at which a person chooses to stop working full time. Legal age to receive federal social security payments is 62 and the amount you get increases if you retire at a later age.

Rich - The state of having a wealth of money.

Risk - The possibility of any investment to go down in value or lose all value, including a business, a stock or a piece of real estate. Risk is the possibility that the result you get is different than the result you expect.

R.O.I. (Return on Investment) - The profit you make on an investment, expressed as a percentage. If you put $1000 into an investment and one year later it's worth $1,100 you have made a profit of $100. Your ROI is your profit ($100) divided by the initial investment ($1000) or 10%.

Salary - A set amount of money you are paid each month for doing your job.

Saving - The act of accumulating something, in this case, the act of saving money.

Savings Account - An account, usually at a bank or credit union, where you put money. This money usually earns interest but cannot be withdrawn by writing a check.

Scarcity - The belief or perception that there isn't enough to go around. An insufficient supply of something.

Simple Interest - Interest paid only on the amount you invest, i.e., principal.

Share (same as a stock certificate) – A certificate representing one unit of ownership in a corporation, mutual fund, or limited partnership.

Social Security - A government program that provides workers and their dependents with retirement income or disability income. The social security tax that is taken out of your paycheck when you are an employee is used to pay for this program.

Supply and Demand - The concept of how prices change depending on how much supply there is of an item and how much demand there is for that item. If the supply is high and the demand is low, the price goes down. If the supply is low and the demand is high, the price goes up.

Stock - A piece of a company. The percentage is determined by the number of shares owned in relation to how many shares exist.

Stock Certificate - A document that represents ownership in a corporation.

Tax - Money that is paid to the government to pay for obligations of the government; things such as road improvement, public education and street cleaning and also welfare, unemployment and disability. There are many kinds of taxes, including income tax, sales tax, gasoline tax, and property tax.

Value - A quality we attach to something we believe is worth something. Something 'has value' or is 'valuable.'

Void - When you write a check and mess it up and need to destroy it you write VOID in the checkbook register or sometimes write VOID on the check itself.

Wall Street - A common name for the financial district in New York City and the street where the New York and American Stock Exchanges are located.

Wants
- The stuff in life we don't necessarily need but have a desire for, i.e., a new bike or car, going on vacation, new clothes or a new stereo.

Wealth
- When you have a lot of something, as in a wealth of friends or a wealth of money.

Withholding Tax
- Amount of an employee's income that an employer sends directly to the federal and state governments as partial payment of an individual's tax liability for the year.

. . . .

Write new **Language of Money** words here as you learn them:

_____
_____
_____
_____
_____
_____
_____
_____
_____
_____
_____
_____
_____
_____

Great job. Keep learning!

Creative Wealth Principles

Review the book or use the Table of Contents to check your answers.

Financial freedom is your _____.

You are the C.E.O. of your life; financial _____ is your responsibility.

Your thoughts, _____ and attitudes determine your wealth potential.

Being _____ is a temporary financial condition, being _____ is a state of mind.

_____ it, _____ it, _____ it down.

Life is an adventure; let _____ be your guide.

To be financially successful, learn the _____ of money.

Money is a _____ to reach your dreams.

Money buys you stuff, not _____.

Make money grow by putting it to _____ for you.

Pay yourself _____.

To create financial freedom, _____ the "energy" of money wisely.

People don't _____ to fail, they fail to _____.

See if YOU can fill in the blanks!

Creative Wealth Principles

It's not how much money you make that's important, it's how much you _____.

If you can't afford it in _____, you can't afford it at all.

Save early, save _____.

Financial success comes from managing _____, not avoiding it.

Interest is only _____ when you're _____ it.

Don't put all your financial _____ into one basket.

Invest with your head, not your _____.

Assets _____ you (produce cash flow), liabilities _____ you.

It is better to tell your money where to _____ than to ask where it _____.

Only _____ money when it's going to _____ you money.

People aren't judged by their _____, but by the sum of their _____.

If you don't know where you're _____ , any road will take you there.

Creating Financial Freedom is simply a matter of developing the right _____.

Financial Wisdom
Puzzle 1 Answers

							S					
							A					
							V					
		S		F	R	E	E	D	O	M		
		U		I								
		M	O	N	E	Y						
				A								
		P	L	A	N		A			I		
W				C			S		K	N	O	W
E		S		I			S			V		
A		T		A			E			E		G
L	I	A	B	I	L	I	T	I	E	S		R
T		T					S			T	O	O	L
H		E									W		

From Page 33

Financial Wisdom
Puzzle 2 Answers

R	I	S	K		P			S				
E					A			T				
S	U	C	C	E	S	S	F	U	L			
P		A			S			F				
O		S			I			F				
N		H			O							
S					N				P			
I			W			H	E	A	D			
B	O	R	R	O	W	A			Y			
I			I			B						
L			T		W	I						
I	N	T	E	R	E	S	T					
T					N	T		S				
Y					T							

From Page 63

Additional Resources for Kids

The 3 Keys to Raising Money Savvy Adults

Author: Elisabeth Donati

Visit **www.CreativeWealthIntl.org** and sign up for our weekly Ezine, **Financial Wisdom with a TWI$T,** full of great tips and information for the whole family.

COST: FREE

Raising money savvy adults can be quite a challenge. Let us help!

Camp Millionaire is a game and activity-based financial education program for kids and teens. We use a powerful teaching methodology called accelerated learning that allows kids to learn by experience.

Your kids will learn how to make, manage and multiply their money wisely, and they'll have a ton of FUN doing it. Imagine your kids learning to be responsible with money BEFORE they leave home and venture out on their own!

Weekend and summer camp events available. Check it out here...

www.CampMillionaire.com

Additional Resources for Kids

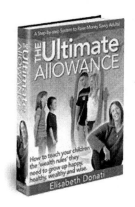

The Ultimate Allowance

Author: Elisabeth Donati

The Ultimate Allowance is the only financial parenting book you need to raise money-savvy adults. A step-by-step system to take the money you already spend ON your children and run it THROUGH them instead. This way they get the practice they need to move out and stay out!

COST: $24.95 (Print or PDF)

Creative Cash for Kids

Want to make sure YOUR kids leave home without YOUR wallet? This simple, easy to use home program was designed for you, the parent, teacher or guardian, with that purpose in mind. We know you don't have a lot of time but you want to make sure your children are prepared to handle the financial aspects of their lives. Program comes with:

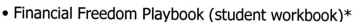

• Financial Freedom Playbook (student workbook)*
• Easy-to-use Parent/Teacher Guide

*Additional student workbooks available

COST: $49 Print/$29 PDF Downloadable

NOTE:

If you'd like to order the Finanical Wisdom Coloring Book in bulk or private label it for your company, please give us a call at 805-957-1024.

Draw Your Own Money Picture!

PRODUCT ORDER FORM

Please fax completed form to **805-957-0125** or mail to **Creative Wealth Intl., LLC, 135 Chapala Street, Santa Barbara, CA 93101**. For info, call 800-928-1928 or 805-957-1024. Please visit us at **CreativeWealthIntl.org**.

PRODUCTS	Cost	Ship/Hand	Qty	Total
Creative Cash for Kids (homeschool/homestudy)	$49.00/set	$6	_____	_____
Includes: Parent/Teacher Guide and Financial Freedom Playbook				
* Additional Playbooks	$14.95/ea.	$1/ea.	_____	_____
Creative Cash at Kids (downloadable PDF file)	$29.00/set	$0**	_____	_____
Financial Wisdom Coloring Book (printed)	$14.95/ea	$3.50	_____	_____
Financial Wisdom Coloring Book (downloadable PDF)	$14.95/ea	$0**	_____	_____
Money Jars (Set of 6 Jars w/Instructions & Labels)	$24.95/set	$10	_____	_____
The Money Game™ (Downloadable) Available 12/15/09	$79.95	$0**	_____	_____
Ultimate Allowance Book ❏ Print ❏ PDF	$24.95/ea.	$5**	_____	_____
Sammy's Music CD	$10.00/ea.	$3	_____	_____
Sammy's Music CD (downloadable)	$10.00/ea.	$**	_____	_____
Sammy's "It's a Habit, Sammy Rabbit!"	$8.95/ea.	$3	_____	_____
Sammy's "Will Sammy Ride the Worlds..."	$8.95/ea.	$3	_____	_____
Life's Little Wealth Principles Cards - Adult*	$19.95/ea.	$3	_____	_____
Life's Little Wealth Principles Journal ❏ Print ❏ PDF	$19.95/ea.	$5**	_____	_____
Wealth Principles Set (Cards & Journal ❏ Print ❏ PDF	$29.95/ea.	$6**	_____	_____

* Youth cards coming soon.

** **Note**: No shipping or sales tax on PDF products.

Total	_____
Tax (8.75% - CA only)	_____
Shipping	_____
Total Due	_____

Name: _____

Shiping Address: _____ Billing Address: _____

City: _____ State: _____ Zip: _____

Phone: _____ Email: _____

Payment Information: ❏ CASH ❏ Check ❏ Visa/Mastercard/American Express

Card Number _____ Ex. Date _____ CVV Code _____

Name on Card _____ Signature _____

CPSIA information can be obtained at www.ICGtesting.com
Printed in the USA
LVOW030243120412

277293LV00001B/19/P